Eberhard Syring · Jörg C. Kirschenmann

HANS SCHAROUN
1893–1972

Outsider of Modernism

TASCHEN

HONG KONG KÖLN LONDON LOS ANGELES MADRID PARIS TOKYO

© 2007 TASCHEN GmbH
Hohenzollernring 53, D-50672 Köln
www.taschen.com

To stay informed about upcoming TASCHEN titles, please request our magazine at www.taschen.com/magazine or write to TASCHEN America, 6671 Sunset Boulevard, Suite 1508, USA–Los Angeles, CA 90028, contact-us@taschen.com, Fax: +1-323-463 4442. We will be happy to send you a free copy of our magazine which is filled with information about all of our books.

Editor ▶ Peter Gössel, Bremen
Project Manager ▶ Swantje Schmidt, Bremen
Layout ▶ Gössel und Partner, Bremen
Translation ▶ Latido, Bremen

Printed in Germany
ISBN 978-3-8228-2778-9

Illustration page 2 ▶ Scharoun in 1946 as head of the Building and Housing Department in front of the placard for the exhibition "Berlin plans – first report".
Illustration page 4 ▶ Pen-and-ink drawing for the "Reflections on the Volkshaus", 1920

Contents

Introduction

Hans Scharoun was a reflective architect. He often accounted for his designs with extensive theoretical explanations that are not easily accessible because of their depth. Scharoun's ideas, expounded in lectures and essays, show a rather extreme independence regarding architecture. His attitude is characterised both by the attempt to achieve a balance between opposites and the perseverance in defending fundamental knowledge against all fads. His central concern focussed on the "essence" of things in social and historical contexts. "Mankind is linked and indebted to the changing time and space, since we create them and are at the same time determined by them; thus the space we live in, is – in its meaning and essence – not of a static, but of a dynamic nature."

This sense of the constant flux of space and time came with an awareness of the processes for change going on in architecture, which ensured that Scharoun never became a representative of an architectural universalism or the so-called International Style. Rather, he considered himself to be an exponent of a cultural area that remained the basis for his architectural creation all his lifetime. This anchoring only gave him the necessary security to anticipate in his draft work the functions that the buildings were intended to serve. In his built work the architect remained true to the functionalist tenets, according to which the design of a building has to be developed from the inside outwards. Accordingly, he shows an ostensible indifference toward the exterior form. The form arises, as Scharoun termed it during a lecture, "inevitably or freely – however one likes to determine." And asked by students whether he was satisfied with the façade of his Berlin Philharmonic, Scharoun is reported to have replied laconically, "Has it got one?"

However, Scharoun was not completely indifferent toward the outside of a building, because he always viewed it as a component of its surroundings, which it must fit into organically. His emphasis on the interior activity is above all a reaction to purely externally-based architectural approaches which aim at prestige and care little about function. "Function – not representation" was already in 1922 Scharoun's motto for a competition entry for a post office in Bremen.

Although his work does not fit the usual stereotyped thinking, it has often been given certain labels. Many see Scharoun above all as an expressionist. When from 1960 on modern architecture was increasingly coming under fire, its expressionist branch was regarded as a new alternative waiting to be discovered. The architect, who as a young man was a member of the expressionist-utopian circle "Gläserne Kette" (Glass Chain), had kept certain stylistic features of expressionism all his life that were starting to find a new appreciation. Even the neoexpressionistic "deconstructivism" of the 1990s seems to have borrowed from Scharoun.

For others Scharoun is the "naval architect". The ship imagery is a distinctive stylistic feature of his buildings, a popular phenomenon of modern architecture of the 1920s. With a critical undertone, the philosopher Ernst Bloch had already stated in reference to this time that the building seen as a ship negates the place where it stands but does not know where it is off to. Along with Le Corbusier, it was probably Scharoun

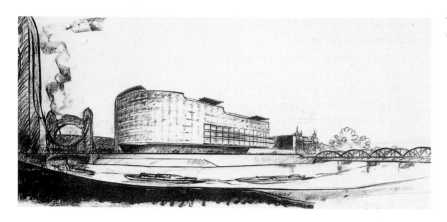

who cultivated this preference most intensely. "One wishes to see something of the
boldness of modern ship structures transferred to the design of houses and thus
hopes to overcome the pettiness and restrictedness of today's housing," Scharoun
wrote around 1928 in an unpublished manuscript. Since he had grown up in the seaport and shipbuilding town of Bremerhaven, this preference for forms had a bio-
graphical aspect as well.

The idea of "organic building" seems to be more important to Scharoun's work
than the formal aspects mentioned above, however. Scharoun referred to the theory of
the architect Hugo Häring he had known since the 1920s. "Organic" does not mean a
preference for biomorphic forms but a principle of design oriented to the structures of
natural life that stands contrary to the dominance of geometric-rationalist thinking and
building. The form of the medieval European town was in most cases the model of
organic building. Häring developed an extensive historico-philosophical theory that
inspired Scharoun. Since he always pursued the principles of functionalism, it is appropriate to speak of an "Organic functionalism". In other words, this refers to giving the
processes within a building their quasi-natural space.

A further characteristic of Scharoun's was his ability to form rooms "as they never
existed before," as a critic exclaimed at the sight of the Berlin Philharmonic foyer. Scharoun had noticed a general tendency in modern aesthetics that culminated in well-
known architectural theoretician Sigfried Giedion's proclamation of a new space-time
conception and broke with the rigid conventions of perspective observation that had
prevailed since the Renaissance.

Scharoun's aesthetics of space was guided by similar thoughts, but unlike Giedion
it had not served as a foundation for a "universal architecture". Rather the room experience in a social sense was relevant to him – as a function of mediation between the
individual and the community. Already in 1925 Scharoun said in a lecture: "All community thoughts culminate in, or better said, become clear by forming the experience between the individual and the space surrounding us." In his explanations of his Mannheim National Theatre design he had tried in 1953 to paraphrase his specific conception of space with the term "aperspective" which he had borrowed from the cultural
philosopher Jean Gebser. The originality of his room creations becomes most evident
in the interior space of the Berlin Philharmonic.

Hans Bernhard Henry Scharoun was born on September 20, 1893 in Bremen. His
father's ancestors originated from Bohemia. When Hans was just a year old the family

moved to Bremerhaven, approximately 65 kilometres down the river Weser, where his father accepted an appointment as the commercial director of a brewery. The young, busy seaport had made a lasting impression upon the adolescent Scharoun, as he remembered years later at the height of his career. In 1967 he said in a lecture in Bremen: "I was a witness to the last years of a tumultuous economic development. (...) The port was the important place of transshipment, the shipment of passengers operated without aircraft competition – so for us boys this all made Bremerhaven and New York into a single unit."

As a schoolboy, Scharoun already stood out because of his talent for drawing. The wish to become an architect arose very early, much to his father's disapproval, who thought there was no money in architecture. Through classmates Scharoun became acquainted with a building contractor family, the Hoffmeyers, who promoted his career aspiration and allowed him early insights into the practical problems of building. Later he married Aenne Hoffmeyer, the daughter in the family.

Among the numerous architectural sketches of Scharoun as a grammar-school pupil the one for a church in Bremerhaven is particularly remarkable– not because of its design, but because of the assertion Scharoun wrote down on the margin of the drawing: "An independent architect should be led not by sensations but by reflections." Remarkably, this motto stood the test in his later conception of his profession and proved afterwards, so to speak, to be a motto for life.

In 1912 Scharoun started to study architecture in Berlin-Charlottenburg, but soon he interrupted his studies. After the outbreak of the First World War he volunteered for military service and was ordered to East Prussian Insterburg for reconstruction. After the war he did not resume studying. He preferred instead to collect practical work experience. In Insterburg he was able to realise his first buildings. It was crucial for the development of his early work that Scharoun was not satisfied with his former teacher Paul Kruchen's approach to building. During this he was already participating in competitions and was engaged in the founding of a society of modern art in Insterburg. Moreover he was looking for connection to artist or intellectual circles in Berlin, which was in that time the most important cultural centre of the modern age between Paris and Moscow.

Scharoun's design as a competition entry for a square at Prenzlau surprisingly won first prize in 1919. For the first time his name was mentioned in specialist publications. The architectural critic Adolf Behne spoke highly about the work of the prospective architect and above all he emphasised his courage in colour. Being a critical companion, inspirer and propagandist of the architectural Modern Movement during the period between the two World Wars Behne was of central significance in Germany. In addition to Bruno Taut and Walter Gropius, he was one of the founding members of the "Arbeitsrat für Kunst" (the Work Council for Art), a union of artists and intellectuals in the revolutionary climate of the immediate post-war period. It was a period of reformation, a period of utopian change. In Germany expressionism was the dominant trend – not only in painting, literature, theatrical and cinematic art but also in architecture. In 1919 Scharoun's name appeared in Berlin in a specialist journal in the "Call for Colour in Construction". He joined the circle around Bruno Taut who had appeared already before the war with the building of his Glass Pavilion at the Cologne Werkbund exhibition as creative brain of the young generation of architects. Shortly afterward Scharoun joined the "Gläserne Kette", a group of artists and architects.

Expressionist architecture-fantasia from the "Gläserne Kette" period

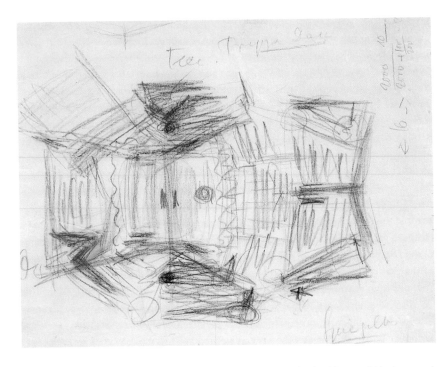

First sketch of the Berlin Philharmonic, 1956

Un
His
abc
In
diff
a d
velv
spa
his

sioι
"se
apa
buil
care
wer
lanc
ope
fror
prir
nee
a hi
rour
com
que
his
roo
but
on
dist

winc
to b
ated
resp
For
poin
sequ

men
pyin
Kett
draft
ness
ing u

A
Arch

starting-point of his dreams to become an architect. In the buildings of his last work one finds many of the principles that were developed in the less successful years. Thus the "room in the centre", the meeting point in the single-family houses of the 1930s had become a typical component of his cultural buildings as well. In the Philharmonic one finds this principle in the fundamental idea "music in the centre".

The work on the basics concerning urban development and dwelling typology of the early 1950s finally bore fruit in numerous housing projects. Because of the great housing shortage, multiple-storey housing became an important subject in the second half of the 1950s. At the Institute for Building and at the Institute for Urban Development at the Technical University Berlin Scharoun had developed an extensive dwelling typology, different systems of development and differing dispositions of rooms. Housing and urban development stood in direct connection for Scharoun. Thus the flat as the smallest element of the city was to assume a special task. In addition to organisational needs, Scharoun wrote in an unpublished manuscript in 1949, "there has to be room within the flat, not only for the family itself, but for the special expectations from life that each member of the family has." The flat should be "the new, freeing background in life"; consequently, it should serve an emancipatory function.

Scharoun in 1963 with fellow architect Werner Weber in the interior room of the Philharmonic

Physical education class at the elementary and secondary modern school in Marl.

Floor plan of the school in Marl

SKIZZE „A"

BETRIEB / NICHT REPRÄSENTATION

1922 ▸ Post office at the station
Unrealised design ▸ Bremen

In 1922 Scharoun produced a design for a competition at his native city of Bremen. It was eliminated after the first round and only the diagram opposite remains preserved. Though one is not able to get a good idea of the suggested structural solution, this paper has often been published. On the one hand it could be the suggestive force of the sketch; on the other hand it can be traced back to the fact that the design was reviewed in a prominent place, in the book "Der moderne Zweckbau" (The Modern Functional Building), written in 1923 by Adolf Behne and published in 1926, one of the earliest sound theoretical tributes to modern architecture.

To understand the extraordinary in Scharoun's work one has to imagine the award presenter's expectations in those days. Behne describes them as follows: "An officially drawn up floor plan combined counter rooms, a parcels room and a postal cheque office under the same roof and behind one façade, for which only the style forms were really sought after."

Scharoun differs from such an idea by "differentiating and articulating" mass, as Behne termed it. Scharoun gave a specific form and site to each functional unit and thus created a group of individually formed structures, corresponding to their special demands. According to Behne, "a building of clear physiognomy comes into being, structured in height, width and length, that answers to the dynamic strain of its functions." The idea of the building is underlined by the motto chosen by Scharoun's motto "function – not representation".

Though Scharoun turned to functionalism after his expressionist utopian period with the "Gläserne Kette" at the beginning of the 1920s, his attitude is shaped through and through by emotional and thus expressive considerations of which even the lines of the paper are eloquent witnesses.

Left page:
View from the station square
To the left is the railway embankment with underpass; in the middle is the round structure of the booking hall; on the right is the head construction of the postal cheque office.

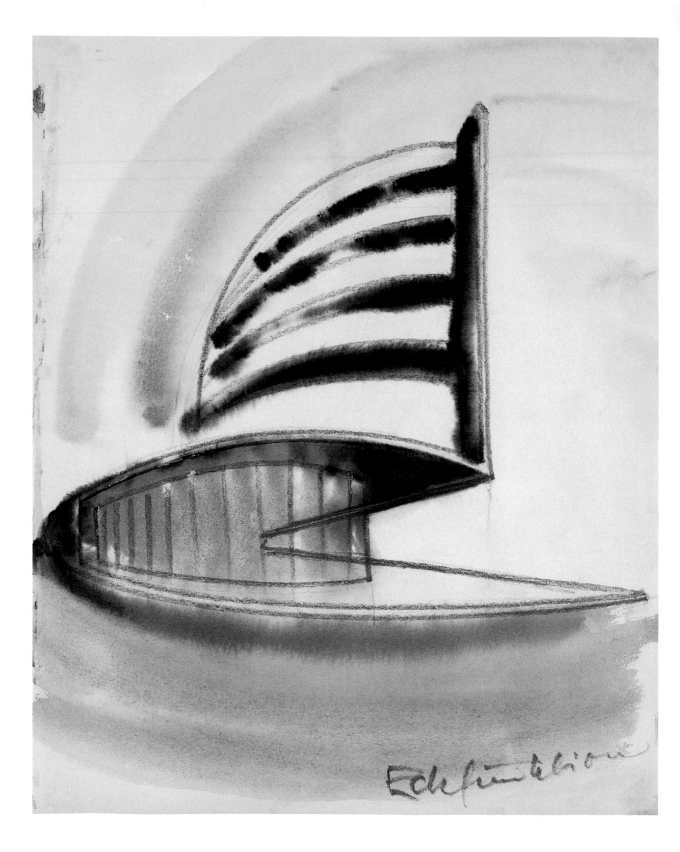

While Scharoun was gaining practical experience with small commissions at the beginning of the 1920s in Insterburg, he was looking for a connecting point to the avantgarde with his competition designs and free studies of form. His studies of form regarding buildings like cinemas, theatres, music and exhibition halls produced around 1922 stand out clearly, both formally and in terms of content, from his contributions to the "Gläserne Kette".

Yet for the critic Adolf Behne, with whom Scharoun corresponded about these works, the difference still was not clear enough. Behne believed to notice echoes of an organic formalism, as in the works of Hermann Finsterlin. Scharoun rejected this in a letter to Behne by making it clear that in these sketches "every line, surface and form can be developed from the requirements of inner essence."

However, one can only anticipate this derivation with the existing sheets, since the corresponding floor plan studies are missing. All in all, it seems that at that time Scharoun was fascinated by the idea that a building is to be created as if by the sedimentation of inner and outer flows of traffic. Therefore places and tasks in the focus of big-city mass traffic had become attractive to him. He was particularly fascinated by the new building project "cinema" and instantly he drew up several designs. One of them he explained to Behne as follows: "Inhaling entrance, straight path to the front, down to the lower theatre-height, a) from here up and distribution within the room, back at the sides b) and at best back out at the rear (at c). Cinema digestion: throat 1st, stomach 2nd, bottom 3rd."

"Theatre"
"Architecture and stage art have to do with the same filling material: with people whose relationship to the building or to the stage gives these things their vitality for the first time."
(Scharoun, 1921)

Left page:
"Eckfunktion" ("Corner-function")
This architectural form was meant to embody the dynamics of modern life in the big city.

"Cinema III"
Scharoun saw cinemas as organisms that at-
tracted people, distributed them and expelled
them again.

The sheets of Scharoun are more reminiscent of the sketches by Erich Mendelsohn
than Finsterlin. They both desire that the dynamics of the modern city be found in its
built form. The formation of building corners played a part of great significance during
this. A corresponding sketch by Scharoun is entitled "Eckfunktion" (corner-function).
In buildings like the block of flats on Hohenzollerndamm or dwelling rows at Siemensstadt Scharoun was later able to realise such corner-functions structurally.

"Cinema V"
The architecture critic Adolf Behne found
Scharoun's designs too farfetched.

1926–1927 ▸ Transportable timber house
German Garden and Industry Exhibition
▸ Legnica, Poland

Plan

Representatives of the new generation of architects demanded repeatedly that the ideas of the "New Building" be presented within the framework of exhibitions. Scharoun too had aspirations to gain both practical experience and fame by building experiments made possible in this surrounding. At the end of the 1920s he was given the opportunity three times: in Legnica, Stuttgart and Wroclaw. In the course of this Scharoun was able to get down to the different problems of housing, a subject he had previously not spent much time on.

For the exhibition in Legnica he developed a transportable timber house which was taken down after the end of the exhibition. In the design and organisation of the house, the prefabrication, internal flexibility and extension had to be given special attention. Functional use and spatial relationships, however, were of particular interest to Scharoun.

The house for a middle-class family was split up into three sections: a working, a living and a sleeping area, creating at the same time two outdoor rooms which were usable in different ways. They enlarge the dining and living room in the centre of the house, which were accentuated as well by greater room height. A maid's room was appointed to the service area, from which the providing for the family was organised.

Scharoun explained his house as a rejection of the formerly customary two, three or four room flats. One has to get from the "room floor plan" to a "requirement floor plan", he said. This idea became especially clear in the spatial relationship between the communicative middle and the children's room in the sleeping section. Open, liveable areas used jointly by the whole family were clearly preferred in questions of design and space to closed rooms like the cabin-like bedrooms. Scharoun thus reached his goal, "to give the house (...) as great a spaciousness within as possible."

Main view
On the left is the housekeeping section; on the right is the sleeping area; between is the somewhat more elevated body of the living area. The house's exterior was kept red and white.

Left page:
The semicircular "sun bath" with a view into the living area
On the left is the wing with the bedrooms, and on the right is the housekeeping area. The Legnica Association of Women's Clubs was involved in the planning.

1926–1927 ▸ "Weißenhofsiedlung"
Werkbund exhibition "The Flat", House 33
▸ Hölzelweg, Stuttgart

Left page:
Living area with a view of the Stuttgart Valley

Entrance side
The sweeping line of the stairwell (right) did not convince every follower of the "new building".

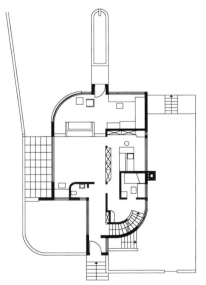

Ground floor plan
An axis in the middle leads from the entrance through the living area into the garden. For Scharoun it was a game of "line versus space".

The Stuttgart Weißenhof housing estate originated in 1927 on the occasion of the exhibition "The Flat" of the German Werkbund. In addition to the established architects and some emerging German ones, Ludwig Mies van der Rohe, who was responsible for the organisation of the development, had given a forum to some rising foreign architects, among them Mart Stam, J.J.P. Oud and Le Corbusier. Thus the international character of the modern architectural movement was emphasised.

The model development was the first public display of modern architecture in Germany and its effect reached beyond the borders. It is typical that Paul Bonatz and Paul Schmitthenner, representatives of the conservative "Stuttgart school", tried to prevent the exhibition. They denigrated the project as an accumulation of flat cubes in unusual narrowness reminiscent of one of the suburbs of Jerusalem. However, Mies van der Rohe was able to have has way at last. The Weißenhof housing estate was intended to be an experiment for new forms of dwelling, rational ways of construction, new designs and construction materials, but mainly it became a big, formal display of the "New Building".

For Scharoun, who until then had stood out above all from his competition designs, this participation was an especially great challenge and lead to a multitude of preliminary designs. The house built on a corner site for a family with two kids was different to the canon of the settlement because it was the only one that fell back on curved shapes. Due to this Scharoun was reproached as a "curve-romantic".

Over a short staircase one reaches the entrance. The living and service areas and – over a step – the bedroom floor are accessible from an entry hall. Large windows open

Above:
**View from the workspace over the living and
dining area onto the terrace**
The sweeping sofa in the centre of the living area
would later become a sort of trademark for Scharoun.

Right:
**The work area can be separated from the
living area with a curtain, if so desired.**

Right page, top:
**Aerial photograph (1927) of the Weißenhof
housing estate**
Scharoun's house is located on the right side
behind the flags.

Right page, bottom:
Isometrics
The stairwell, the living room border and the garden
wall form a semicircle that prevents the body of
the structure from being strictly right-angled.

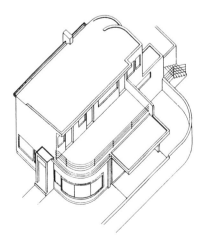

the living area to the outside. The dining space is connected to the covered terrace by a room-high glazing. From the sofa one gets a view across the Stuttgart valley, and the working area opens to the garden. Service and dining area are situated on the same level. Two steps up, on the garden level the living and working area is visually separated from this by a mid-high built-in element without interrupting the flow of space. In the differentiated opening of the living area to the external space a motif is perceptible, which is characteristic of Scharoun's later work.

1928 ▸ Weite House
Unrealised design

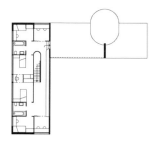

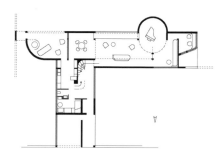

Above:
Top floor plan

Below:
Ground floor plan

Left page:
View over the front garden
In the background is the two-storey wing with the entrance and the sleeping area above it. On the right is the extensive living space with the sun terrace on the flat roof.

With this design, a competition entry, Scharoun was engaged again fundamentally in the subject of the "middle class house with service", which means one need not take into consideration the concrete desires of a client. As stated in the invitation, "a single-family house that corresponds to today's requirements of hygiene, a private house of the young world, of the new age" was sought. Unconstrained by a special site or plot shape Scharoun was able to explore his ideas of modern dwelling.

The starting-point for the organisation of the two-storey buildings was the skilled arrangement of three functional areas: a service area, a living area and a sleeping area. The angular floor plan shows a two-storey wing running diagonally to the street with a garage and services on the ground floor and bedrooms above. Thus the design sets the large single-storey living wing at a distance from the street. Low walls enclose the house from the street and it opens to the landscape with a generous gesture.

One enters the building from the narrow side facing the street next to the garage and is led – supported by the location of the staircase – into the elongated living room that is characterised by a greater room height and a great double-glazed window with plants in between. The communicative centre of the room is emphasised by the placement of two sofas. A separated study faces westward, and an oval-shaped music area can be separated visually just as well by a curtain, as can the square eating area, which connects to a covered terrace on the east side. Dining space and terrace again are connected to the kitchen.

The individual, cabin-like rooms of the parents and children on the upper floor are accessible from a corridor with a built-in cupboard. At the southern end of the corridor there are the children's territory and the access to a sun terrace; the sewing room is situated at the other end of the corridor. Both bathrooms are shared – one by father and son and the other by mother and daughter.

Left:
View from the side facing away from the street with the semicircle of the music area in the foreground

Right:
View from the dining space into the long axis of the living area

1928–1929 ▸ Hostel

Werkbund exhibition "Dwelling and Workroom"
▸ ul. Kopernika, Wroclaw, Poland

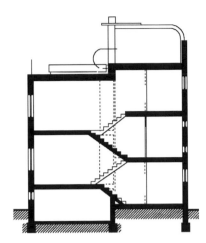

Cross-section of the wing with the single-bedroom flats
The upper and the lower flat open up from one corridor (right, middle storey). The sun-terrace is located on the roof.

Right:
Front area on the park side with garden restaurant
The two narrow strips on the windows (top right) are the hall lights, placed uncommonly high and deep.

Following the success of the Stuttgart Werkbund exhibition "The Flat", the Werkbund exhibition "Dwelling and Workroom" took place in the summer of 1929 in Wroclaw. In contrast to the internationally organised Stuttgart exposition, the Wroclaw exposition could be carried through only on the condition that it represented the whole range, particularly the local interpretation of traditionalist building. Thus the Werkbund housing development obtained a somewhat heterogeneous outward appearance.

Scharoun's hostel was certainly the most important building of the exposition. By its sheer size and form alone, it dominated the northern part of the exhibition area that bordered on a park not far from the Jahrhunderthalle designed by Max Berg. Scharoun took up residential buildings as his theme, which touched on his apartment buildings being built in Berlin at the same time. In comparison to those at Wroclaw, the structural form resulted primarily from reflections on the coherence of the inner functions.

The building is divided into two residential wings. The longer and straighter one contains one-person flats, the shorter and curved one two-person flats. A communal area with a large hall is inserted between both wings. The three structural parts are curved against each other in a way creating an almost S-shaped figure, forming two opposite concave front areas, used outside as a shady open-air restaurant, inside as a cosy yard.

Scharoun uses the arrangement of the small flats in rows as an opportunity to emphasise the horizontal by uninterrupted balustrades and rows of windows. The 48 dwelling units are arranged in a way that in both wings stacked flats, staggered at half-

Left page:
View onto the yard
On the left, the wing with the two-person flats can be seen which incorporates the dining hall below it.

33

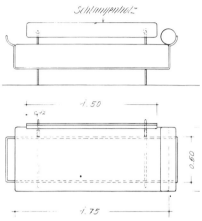

Part of the furniture was designed by Scharoun himself

Above:
The central hall is located between the two residential wings

Left, bottom:
Ascent to the sun-terrace

Right, bottom:
Dining hall

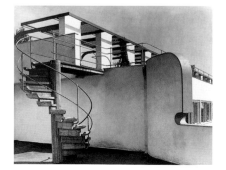

Top:
The living area of a single-bed flat with a view of the settlement
Bottom:
Living area of a two-bedroom flat with a front loggia

storey intervals that lie on top of each other are accessible via only one corridor. This way Scharoun achieves two-sided lighting and visual generosity even with minimal ground space. A loggia is situated off the two-person flats, and for the smaller flats, a generous sun-terrace on the roof is available.

Sun terrace and yard

"One wishes to see something of the boldness of modern ship structures transferred to the design of houses and thus hopes to overcome the fussiness and narrowness of today's housing."
(Scharoun, 1928)

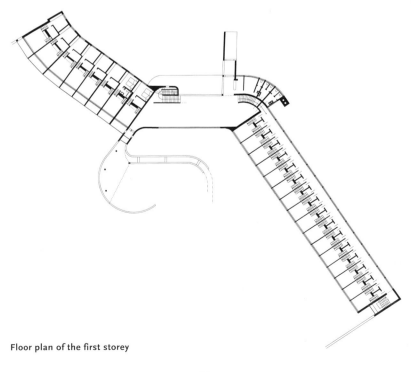

Floor plan of the first storey

1929–1930 ▸ Apartment building
Hohenzollerndamm, Berlin

A clinker base and a jutting-out eave contrast with the dominating smartness of the white façade.

The corner house is the second apartment building Scharoun planned for the building contractor Georg Jacobowitz in Berlin. One year prior he had implemented a similar building project on Kaiserdamm. However, in both cases Scharoun's contribution was restricted to the outer form. The floor plans had been predetermined. Such form-making from outwards actually contradicted the creed of the architect, according to which buildings are to be planned from the inside to the outside. Nonetheless in both buildings he had success with distinctively urban architectural symbols. The house on Hohenzollerndamm is impressive due to its dynamic corner solution with the stretched out, circular loggias.

Both blocks of flats are first results from a series of attempts in which Scharoun tackled new forms of residences for the "big-city type", as he once termed it – in other words, small-sized and minimal-sized flats for the needs of the growing number of working single persons and childless couples in the 1920s.

Ideally, such a house would look more like a hotel then a usual apartment house. Practical built-in furniture would reduce the individual portion of the furnishings to a minimum and even the cooking facilities in the flat would be superfluous if a restaurant in the house took over the food supply. This was certainly not intended here.

Even the version as a 22.5 metre deep double row with a narrow courtyard covered with glass intensifies the impression that with this project the economic calculation got preference over the structural ideal.

Standard storey floor plan

Left page:
The corner of the building is effectively emphasised by bold, projecting, gondola-like loggias.

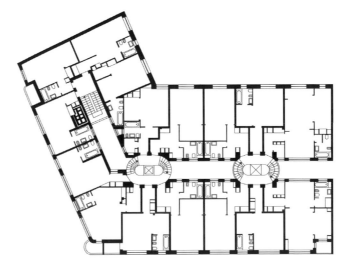

1929–1931 ‣ Siemensstadt housing estate
Jungfernheideweg and Mäckeritzstraße, Berlin

This housing estate project was initiated by City Architect Martin Wagner and sponsored by a Berlin special programme for flats of minimal size established in 1928. For the general site plan there was an internal competition among the prevailing members of the architects' association "Der Ring", then the most important organisation of modernists in Germany. According to the newest erudition in housing development a housing estate was best built in rows. The decision went to Hans Scharoun's design. In addition to Scharoun, who implemented the three southern rows that mark the entrance to the housing estate, as well as the site plan, Walter Gropius, Otto Bartning, Hugo Häring, Paul Rudolf Henning, and Fred Forbat had designed the other buildings.

The Siemensstadt site plan is regarded as one of the best examples in modern architecture of a creative, manifold monotony that avoids contact with the Zeilenbau principle. "The plan could have been a reference for the Zeilenbau-housing estates after the Second World War, but nobody paid any attention," was the subsequent judgement of the well-known architecture historian Julius Posener. In Scharoun's skilfully adapted plan for the situation given, long rows alternate with short ones, as do straight ones with curved ones, ones facing the street with ones facing away from the street, and ones facing north-south with ones facing east-west. Thus a most differentiating structure of rooms comes into being that allows no room for boredom. With its maximum amount of differentiation the Siemensstadt is regarded as the structural antithesis to the rather schematic developments like Karlsruhe-Dammerstock or Frankfurt-Westhausen.

Site plan

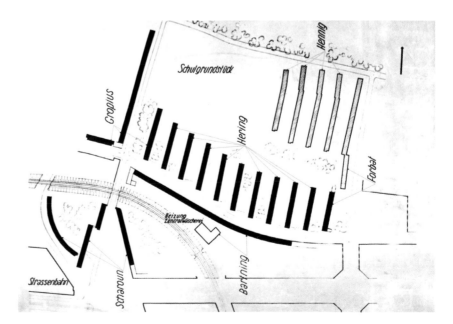

Left page:
Clear-cut balconies characterise the middle of these three rows of buildings, called "Armoured Cruiser".

"Armoured Cruiser"
The extremely thin, homogeneous windshield of the loggias contributes decisively to its suggestion of a ship.

Scharoun's group of buildings is flanked to the south by an older block construction. Scharoun formally agreed to this handicap by positioning his structures in squares, facing the street. Consequently a triangular entrance square was designed. Yet in doing so Scharoun did by no means do without the advantages of modern row construction like maximal orientation to the sun and to green area.

For the three rows Scharoun created types of flats cut especially for the site and alignment. The western row, which swung convex to the street (flat type B), got its distinctive silhouette by loggias which merge into units with stairwells sticking out from the line of façades.

The middle row (flat type A) is surprising due to a change of alignment of the flats to the street and courtyard. With their striking, dynamically projecting balconies they form the most marked structural part and in the vernacular got the name "armoured cruiser". By means of a projection in this row and the funnel-shaped next row attached to the east the architect formed a gate-like narrowness as a passage to the northern half of the housing estate. The C flat-type of the eastern row is distinguished by a continuous living and dining area which is lit from two sides.

Scharoun himself moved with his wife into one of the C type small flats he designed, where he lived until 1960.

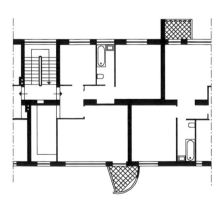

Floor plan of a type A flat
The flats alternate facing the yard and the street.

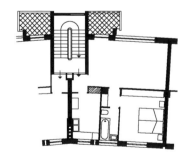

Floor plan of a type B flat
Loggias and a stairway form a single unit.

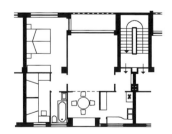

Floor plan of the east row of Type C
Hans and Aenne Scharoun lived in an flat like this until 1960.

Above:

The row on Mäckeritzstraße (type B) is conjoined with its neighbouring row (right), making a block-shaped figure.
Its curved form is animated by the prominent relief of the wall and the "stair towers" as well as by the play of horizontal and vertical elements.

Left:

View into Scharouns' flat
In the background is the workspace with the window. Scharoun received the painting (right) from Lyonel Feiniger in 1920.

1930–1933 · Schminke House
Kirschallee, Löbau

Left page:
The north-east corner of this building is the point of culmination in this architectural composition, both in the way in which the interior paths lead as well as in the shaping of the body of the building.

The house for the pasta manufacturer Fritz Schminke and his wife Charlotte is probably Scharoun's most famous work from the period between the wars. It is mentioned by many critics in the same breath with the Villa Savoye by Le Corbusier or the Villa Tugendhat by Ludwig Mies van der Rohe. The construction site joins the factory site to the north. The site lies on a northwards sloping hill with an attractive view. The client's father had wanted to build a villa at this site in 1916 but he could not actualise it because of the First World War. A landscaped garden already existed from this period. For Scharoun it was now sound on the one hand to stage the view of the landscape, taking the existing garden complex into account, and on the other hand to find the maximum orientation towards the side facing the sun without moving the building too much toward the factory.

The sketch was produced in intensive collaboration with the clients, who were interested in modern architecture. By 1930, the draft design was already complete. Because of financial problems in that economically difficult period, however, the construction was delayed until 1933, which strengthened the dialogue between the clients and the architect. Thus a very specific building was able to come into being, with Scharoun bringing in his newest knowledge about modern housing. This was exhibited by the way in which the living, service and sleeping areas were attached.

The structure of the steel frame construction is a two-storey cross-bar lying parallel to the slope, running east-west and containing the living area below and bedrooms upstairs. At the end walls it is penetrated by parts of the building that are twisted approximately 30° and run parallel to the boundaries. On the west side there is the service area, on the east side the conservatory with terrace. The difficult room arrangement develops out of a play with these two directions. Visitors enter the building from the

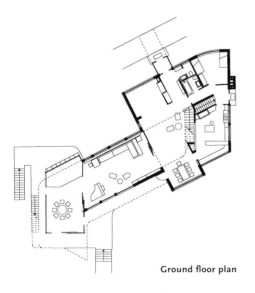

Ground floor plan

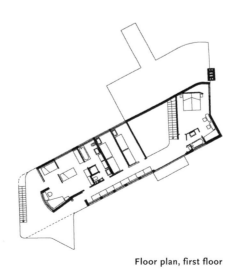

Floor plan, first floor

View from the garden side
With its rustic materials, the garden architecture of Hermann Mattern sets a contrast that increases the effect of the building.

south side, where the living and service areas border. The axis of entry, emphasised by a towering canopy, sweeps rectangular to the main wing. Following the axis, one reaches the two-storey entrance hall at the side, which joins to the playing area to the south and to the dining area to the north. One's first look goes to the main stair that is taken up in the twisting of the service wing.

Due to this change in direction the visitor is led unaware to the main axis of the ground floor, which leads from the entrance hall immediately to the living room, which fluidly passes over into the conservatory. In the succession of these layers of rooms their boundaries become more transparent and brighter. In the conservatory, with its big plant basin, building and garden finally seem to enter each other. At the end of this axis, a whitewashed outdoor stairway running parallel to the main stairway introduces a further change in direction: to the lower terrace level and to the opening panorama.

In addition to this leading of view and movement, effectively staged by means of changes in direction, one's experience of the rooms in the Schminke House is also determined by the play with light, shadow and reflection, transparency and screening, and colour and form. The amazing variety of forming elements, materials and colours is visually structured by the limitation to simple geometric patterns, mostly squares and circles.

In contrast to the generous flow of space in the living area, the sleeping area in the upper floor is of a consciously Spartan design. Only the airy sundeck with a bold cantilever is a particular element. On the west side there is a guest room.

Conservatory with plant basin
The colour picture was taken after the restoration of the house in the 1990s.

Below:
Living area and conservatory seem to penetrate each other.
The whitewashed outdoor steps direct one's glance to the expanding landscape panorama.

Bottom:
The same view in the evening with closed curtains

The Schminke House is the culmination and endpoint of Scharoun's dynamic "white modernism" phase, in which he liked to play with suggestions of steamships. Coming through the house and landscape room, already one sees the proclamation of his further development.

North side
The house's skilled gradation of depth is evident here as well as the interplay of surfaces structured in large and small parts.

Left:
Entryway with dining area (right), children's playing area and stairway to the top floor

Bottom left:
The parents' sleeping area and day room with a view onto the sun deck

Bottom right:
This corridor of Spartan dimensions in the sleeping area is brought to life with geometric symbols.

1932–1934 ‣ Mattern House
Florastraße, Potsdam

Scharoun had met his client, landscape architect Hermann Mattern, when he designed the garden for the Schminke House which was completed in 1933. A lasting, intensive collaboration arose out of it.

Under a low-pitched roof the angular designed house opens in manifold ways to the garden and to the sun. The western wall curves outwards, ending with a slanting, rustically built closure. On the inside this curving is filled by a generous custom-made sofa. It is a requisite that can be regarded as a trademark, so to speak, for Scharoun's residential buildings of the 1930s. Outside, the curving defines a seat in the setting sun. The living room, openly linked with dining area and study, gets an extensive glazing like a conservatory.

The sleeping area is accessible separate from the entry hall. The beds are arranged like bunk beds, with little space. Thus enough room for a spacious indoor children's playground remains that one can expand to a covered terrace with a glass sliding door.

Even with this small house Scharoun succeeded in connecting functional spaces within and distinct spaces outdoors so that an extraordinary interrelation of spaces could come into being.

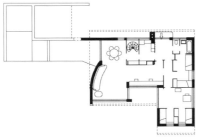

Ground floor plan

Bottom left:
The workspace is located between the living area and the sleeping area.

Bottom right:
The sofa is made to fit the curved west wall.
In the background the dining area

1934–1935 ▸ Baensch House
Höhenweg, Berlin

As a modernist, Scharoun was very restricted in his fields of activity during the Nazi rule. Nevertheless, he managed to implement a few residential buildings "of fundamental importance", as he termed it. The regalia of modern architecture – steel, glass, machine aesthetics – fell under the verdict of the Nazis during house construction. In such small commissions for single-family houses that saved Scharoun at the end of 1930s professionally he had to concentrate on the floor plan and the landscape lest his creative potential go unused. Houses were thus built that show characteristics of traditionalism externally, with walls and pitched roofs, but their ground floor layout and interior room development are experimental and extremely innovative.

So is the Baensch House, where the entire floor plan is conceived of as a dwellingscape, unfolding in the shape of a fan, nestling up to the sloping plot with an attractive view of a riverside. The cardinal point of the three segments of the fan is the oval-shaped dining space. It is the functional end of the service wing, which is connected over the open living hall to a separable, opposite lying study. The third fan segment, emphasised by its approximately three-step depression, joins the living area that opens to the landscape with a vast concave window wall. One can find some elements typical of Scharoun's single-family houses. There is a music space emphasised by a circular, opaque window (bullseye), a large window as a kind of a small greenhouse and – centrally-placed – the generous sofa, from which one can best enjoy the distant view across the landscape.

Like in the Schminke House, the upper floor with bedrooms is kept very modest and is dominated by a large sun terrace that copies the sweep of the living area.

Top:
The garden side of the house shows an attractive silhouette.
Above the bulge of the living area is a spacious terrace, from which a free-hanging staircase (right) leads directly into the garden.

Above:
View from the living room into the work area
The curved sofa is fitted to the room; the round window marks the music space.

Right:
Ground floor plan

Left page:
From the terrace one can enjoy the view of the Havel landscape.

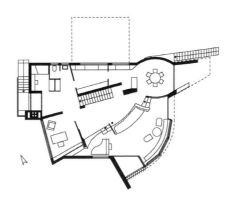

1939–1945 ‣ Visionary sketches

Left page:
Untitled watercolour
The stream of people indicated by the dots are reminiscent of the old expressionist dream of the "Stadtkrone", the great cultural building as a symbol of community.

When in 1967 the Berlin Academy of the Arts, whose president of many years' standing was Hans Scharoun, dedicated an extensive exhibition to the architect, a series of papers appeared for the first time in public that Scharoun had composed during the Second World War. Scharoun said in the exhibition catalogue: "From the outbreak of war to the surrender, drawings, watercolours and sketches arose, day after day. They were done out of survival instinct as well as from the compulsion to take up the question of the coming form."

All together in Scharoun's assets there are nearly 250 registered watercolours, pen and pencil drawings from these years. They do not exceed DIN A 4 format and for this reason could be collected inconspicuously in the cellar. The architectural subjects exhibited show quite a lot of relations: On the one hand there are historic models from Piranesi to the Russian Constructivists, who could have inspired Scharoun; on the other hand his later built work seems to appear already as formal anticipations in some papers.

The depicted buildings, which are mostly not marked in detail, are usually public buildings (theatres, churches, halls, lookout towers). Here Scharoun's longing for great symbols of community is clearly to be seen, and he shows no inhibitions about monumental forms, as one can see in his built work. In contrast to his built work, many of his representations stick to a strong emotional trait, which may have something to do with the personal situation of their creator.

The motif of crowds ascending a series of almost endless staircases whose destination is hidden is almost obligatory. Scharoun was engaged frequently with the indirect lighting of buildings in added section sketches. Works and details of a lightly poetic character are rather in the minority. The sheet "Dachwölkchen – beweglich" (Roof clouds – mobile) is an example.

Bottom left:
Untitled watercolour

Bottom right:
"Roof clouds – mobile", watercolour

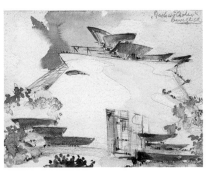

1951 ▸ Basic primary and secondary school
Unrealised design ▸ Darmstadt

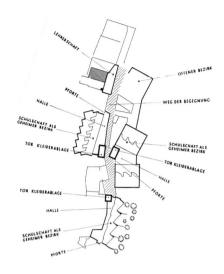

Floor plan diagram

Left page:
Model photo
The backbone of this lengthy attachment is the "meeting path".

The design was produced on the occasion of the "Darmstadt Conversations" whose central theme in 1951 was entitled "Man and Space". The point of reference was the 50th anniversary of the first exhibition of the Darmstadt artist's colony at Mathilden-höhe. To give a concrete reference to the three-day conference, to which prominent philosophers like Martin Heidegger und José Ortega y Gasset were invited as well, "master buildings" had been designed by selected architects which were to be discussed in the framework of the event. It was overwhelmingly about public building projects, which were cut out for locations in Darmstadt. An implementation was promised on the part of the city. Scharoun's unrealised sketch for a school had gained the most attention and left a strong influence on the school building debate in Germany.

The deeply intellectual work from which Scharoun generated the structure is impressive. The school as an institution possessed for him likewise a mediating function between individual and society as well as between family and city. The school is planned after the model of a town to make possible the experience of the relationships between these poles. It comprises individual sections that were developed according to the peculiarities of the pupils' age and which are linked by an internal street, called the "meeting path". The rooms for the youngest pupils (grades 1 to 3) have a partly sheltering, cave-like or nest-like character, but face the sun too. The premises of the middle school (grades 4 to 6) are "unequivocally arranged and brought into a safely limited connection with outside world and group world," as the architect explained. The section of the upper grades (grades 7 to 8) is intended to advocate the development of personal identity within the community. The so-called "open area" is the central meeting place within the building, but serves as a mediation point between the school and the urban quarter, too.

The tendency to a structural realisation, corresponding to the nature and exactly comprehending the respective task was the subject of heated discussion at the conference. To many there seemed to be too much subjectivity in the architectural interpretation of the requirements. However, Scharoun's principle of a deepened engagement with the task of building had incontestably produced a highly innovative architecture.

Right:
Group "A" room perspective sketch
"The group 'A' is spiritually creative and playful", said Scharoun in his explanatory report.

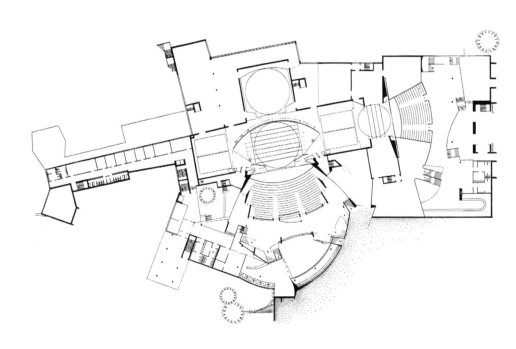

1952–1954 ▸ Kassel National Theatre
Unrealised design

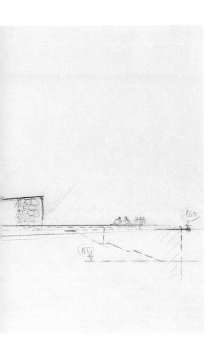

Scharoun had produced the competition design together with landscape architect Hermann Mattern, with whom he had worked since the 1930s. The Kassel National Theatre is probably the most famous unrealised project of the architect. The unanimity is remarkable with which the jury awarded the work first place in 1952. Even conservative jury-chairman Paul Bonatz highly praised the work.

As was customary in Scharoun's process of "form-making" the sketch is based on two principles of investigation. On the one hand, the scenic characteristics and historical elements of the location are investigated; on the other hand, the building task is considered on the basis of its innovative potential and whether its forms are contemporarily appropriate.

The Kassel sketch is strongly influenced by an idea of cultural landscape. This concerns the integration of the building into the cityscape as well as the interior room design itself. It was due to the concept of urban landscape that Scharoun cancelled the former shape of the disproportionally large looking Friedrichplatz by consciously moving the theatre block from the central axis to the brink, thus staging the view to the landscape.

One of the greatest architectural scandals of the 1950s was linked to the Kassel project. Although work had been started in 1955, the project was dropped for invalid reasons and the theatre was realised according to plans of a local architect. During his famous lecture "Democracy as a Building Client" Adolf Arndt paid attention to this occurrence in 1960: "After the foundation stone had been laid with great pomp the opponents presented their apparent technical and financial objections. (...) The financial department of the state building authorities put the design aside and did something of its own. Ultimately it required three times the million dollar amount. The (...) Kasselers call the failure with grim humour the 'material testing department'."

Left page, top:
Sketch of the exhibition design: outside view from the urban side.
The "body structure's reference to the mountainous landscape in the background via the shape of the stage area" was for Scharoun "an optical means of integration".

Left page, bottom:
Floor plan of the parquet storey with stage level and entrance to the sloped theatre

Left:
Views of the theatre from the Karlsaue
This building was intended to define the transition from city to the park anew.

Right:
Sketch of the urban area idea
Scharoun: "It is about the resumption of the relationship to the landscape."

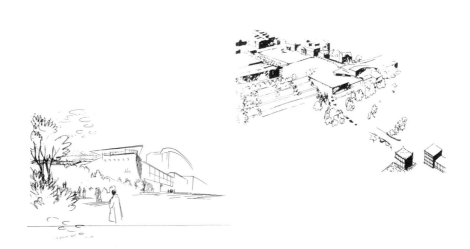

1954–1959 ▸ Romeo and Juliet
Residential development
▸ Schozacher Straße and Schwabbacher Straße, Stuttgart

The Juliet-Building rises twelve storeys high dynamically and expressively

With these buildings Scharoun was able to implement his first post-war project. Executed in collaboration with Stuttgart architect Wilhelm Frank, the complex first of all provided a distinct mixture of housing. The unusual floor plans, above all the circular building "Juliet", met with no approval from the Office for Subsidised Housing. The property developer decided to plan all 186 flats as private flats.

Within the conventional surroundings with rows of double pitched roofs, both buildings co-ordinated in height operate like urban accents, around which the centre of the settlement had developed. "Juliet", on the west side, rises to its height in three steps starting at five storeys, than eight up to twelve. On the east side the nineteen storey solitaire "Romeo" takes up this development of height structurally. The most distinct exterior features are the tapered balconies that stretch to the sun. These give the structures, together with the projecting roofs of the stacked storeys, a sheer dynamic, almost expressive effect.

"Juliet", with its dexterous circular arrangement of the floor plan and southward orientation, demonstrates that even the larger flats are accessible via an open gallery. In the building "Romeo" six flats per floor are accessible via an L-shaped corridor lit from two sides.

As a result of the success of the co-ordinated buildings, Scharoun was able to implement in the Stuttgart area yet more blocks of flats with further-developed systems of entering the flats and floor plan versions, for example the double high-rise building named "Salute" at Stuttgart-Fasanenhof and the "Orplid" complex at Böblingen. The block of flats on Zabel-Krüger-Damm in Berlin can be looked at as a continuation of this line of development.

Right:
Floor plans of the buildings and their standard storeys with their various realisations:
Semicircular pergola (Juliet) and L-shaped interior hallway (Romeo)

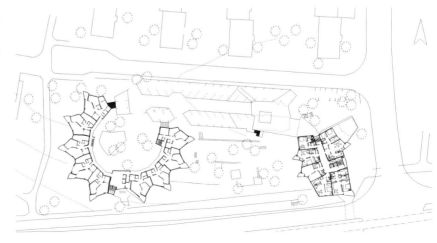

Left page:
Entrance area of the Romeo high-rise

1954–1961 ▸ Charlottenburg-Nord
Housing estate ▸ Goebelplatz and Heilmannring, Berlin

Right:
Floor plan
The Heilmannring divides the settlement. Thus the original concept of the "courtyard houses" can only partially be seen.

▦	3-storey
▤	4-storey
▨	5-storey
▥	6-storey
▦	8-storey
▥	9-storey
▥	11-storey

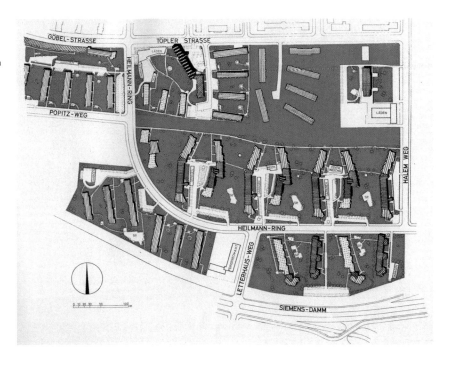

This housing estate, the biggest designed by Scharoun, joins in the east the Siemens-stadt housing estate from the late 1920's, whose site plan was also produced by him. The sketch is derived from his urban concepts for the rebuilding of Berlin after the Second World War. In 1946 Scharoun had presented as City Architect the so-called "Kollektivplan", according to which Berlin should have been transformed to an urban scenic structured Bandstadt. "Dwelling-cells" were intended as urban basic units, housing estates for approximately 5000 inhabitants. As head of the Institute for Building Industry Scharoun had developed such a housing estate as an example for the East Berlin district Friedrichshain in 1949. However, this building project fell victim to the wide tree-lined Boulevard Stalinallee.

Charlottenburg-Nord too was designed as a complete "Wohnzelle" (living-cell) in an ideal plan of 1955. In addition to different types of residential buildings, ranging from chain houses to dense multi-storey blocks, diverse communal facilities and public institutions were part of them, among them a school taking up the Darmstadt design of 1951 for the basic primary and secondary school. "Courtyard houses" were to form the southern end of the housing estate. In the end, only this part could be realised according to Scharoun's plans, and even then only in reduced form. A collecting road intersects the "courtyard houses" silhouettes, loosely integrated into the landscape.

The original idea of room structure is above all recognisable in the area north of the street. Here rows of buildings are situated, which are folded many times and variously

Left page:
The settlement's appearance shows the variety of flats.

63

View over the "courtyard houses"
The highest flats are studios.

graduated in length and height development, including a great number of different types of flats. The rows are shaped in a way so that there is a switch from concave gaps to convex ones. The concave space formulates a forecourt from which all entrances are accessible. The convex gap is more scenery-oriented. A cross-bolt effect of the rows is avoided by a footpath that provides a short link between the courtyard houses.

Scharoun himself moved out his Siemensstadt flat to one of the studio flats at Charlottenburg-Nord.

Floor plan of the southern head construction of the rows lying south of the Heilmannring.

Studio flat on the top floor of the highest rows
Rising rooflines and slanted windows characterise the studio flats. Scharoun himself lived and worked in such an flat starting in 1960.

The studio flat on the top floor offers the best view over the settlement.

1955–1962 ▸ Geschwister-Scholl School
Holtgrevenstraße, Lünen

Scharoun's design for the municipal girls' grammar school specialising in modern languages at Lünen (Westphalia) followed the criteria established with his Darmstadt design for a basic primary and secondary school and adapted them to the local conditions. The design is also influenced by the idea of the school's mediating function between the private and individual on one hand and society on the other hand. A class community becomes a "second family" that lets one experience "the essence of a social family," the architect explained on the occasion of a lecture at the Triennale in Milan in 1960. Accordingly, Scharoun called the eighteen classroom units "school-dwellings".

Similar to the Darmstadt sketch different types of classrooms were found for the three age groups, according to their specific developmental stage. All classrooms have a stretched hexagonal-shaped floor plan, to which a niche-like annexe (group room), a lobby (cloakroom) and a courtyard for open-air teaching are attached. The rooms for the youngest schoolgirls have an extroverted alignment, corresponding to the prevailing naive lack of distance of this age group towards the environment. On the contrary, the placing of the rooms for the middle age group is marked by isolation, parallel to the more introverted behaviour, which is characteristic for this developmental stage. Scharoun awarded an elevated position within the building to the oldest schoolgirls. Their classrooms are on the upper floor, and terraces are put in place for instruction outside.

A 100 metre long break hall is the spatial backbone of the school. Two ground floor class wings and specialised science rooms are attached at the north and south, respectively. The irregular pentagon of the assembly hall joins in the west, near the main entrance, a with fluid transition to the break hall.

Above:

On the street side are the science laboratories at the bottom and the group of rooms for work and art instruction at the top.

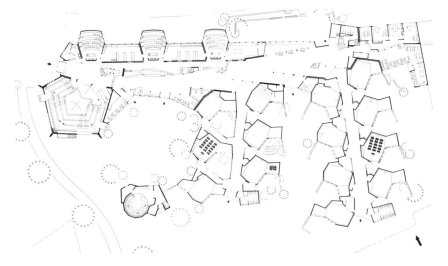

Ground floor plan

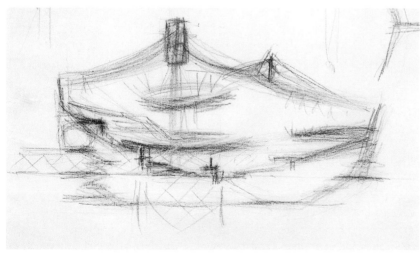

1956–1963 ▸ Philharmonic
Herbert-von-Karajan-Straße, Berlin

View from the Southwest, 1964
The Philharmonic was the first building stone of the new culture forum at the edge of the Tiergarten.

Left page:
First sketch, 1956

When the Philharmonic was inaugurated in October 1963, Scharoun had already celebrated his 70th birthday. With this building he gained for the first time the international recognition that had been denied him for years because important and competition-winning sketches were not realised. The first ever commission for Scharoun that resulted from an award at a competition was the winning design for the Philharmonic in 1956.

The originally envisaged site of the Philharmonic lay in the centre of West Berlin. After the "Capital Berlin" competition of 1958, it was decided to establish a new "cultural forum" to the south-east of Berlin-Tiergarten. The Philharmonic was to become the first building of this complex.

The fundamental principle of Scharoun's design is as simple as it is brilliant. Starting with the observation that people always spontaneously form a circle around the musicians when music is performed, the Philharmonic is the attempt to transpose this principle into a concert hall. "Music in the centre" was the motto of the design, in which the metaphor became the shape of a room. The result is a typological innovation for building. For the first time a concert hall was designed where audience and musi-

Outside view 1963
Due to financial reasons, plans for outside panelling had to be abandoned. The surface was made of exposed concrete painted white and ochre.

Left:
Outside view today
A gold anodised aluminium panelling was added in the 1980s.

cians were not across from each other. The orchestra is positioned in the centre of the room instead, not in the geometric middle, yet nonetheless completely enveloped by their audience, which is arranged at terraced segments of circles. Despite the monumental scale of the hall, an intimate atmosphere is created, and the hall has excellent acoustics, too.

Yet the Philharmonic comes to life just as well with the contrast between the concentric heart of the hall and the fluid roomscape of the foyer, which is situated under the body of the hall. More and more deep stratas open up to the view, making it difficult to estimate the actual size of the room. At intermission, it offers relaxed promenading as well as the highly enjoyable observation of the other visitors' flow of movement in the room. Dutch architect Jacob Behrend Bakema positively commented on the foyer, "that the entries and exits, stairs, galleries and lifts, the guidance of the visitors from the street to the seats ... appear like a piece of city building. My wish is that his design principles be true for whole cities." Yet quite in the sense of organic functionalism, the exterior form is hardly the mirror image of the interior activity.

East lookout
The homogeneously flowing exterior layer is only penetrated in a few spots.

Ground floor plans
Left: main podium and music foyer
Middle: upper foyer
Right: upper tier of the concert hall

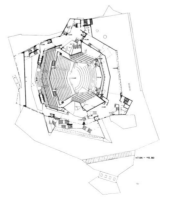
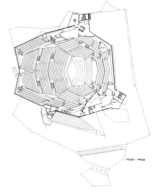

Above and right page:
The flowing roomscape of the foyer forms an antipole to the concentric space of the hall.

View into the concert hall
Herbert von Karajan: "I don't know of any existing
concert hall in which the seating problem is as
ideally solved as it is in this design."

Below:
**View into the foyer during a concert
intermission in 1964.**

Cross-section looking west

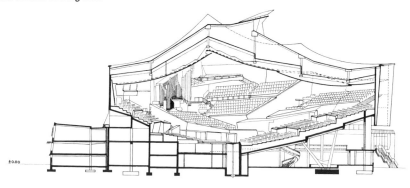

±0.00

1960–1971 ▸ School building
Westfalenstraße, Marl

Left page:
View into the break hall
The break hall and the assembly hall together form the centre of the school, the "room in the middle".

Right:
"School flat" of the middle age-group
The recessed group room is attached to the left side of the stretched hexagonal classroom. On the left next to the blackboard is the exit to the playground.

"School flats" of the lower grades
The hexagonal classrooms have circular skylights.

Parallel to the completion of the girl's secondary school at Lünen, Scharoun was concerned with another school at Marl (Westfalen), a town also on the northern border of the Ruhr region. He was commissioned to build a school building on a slightly undulating ground, part of an area of suburban development. Here he was once again able to implement architecturally his distinct idea of a contemporary school aware of its social role. Scharoun formulated his central ideas in his speech at the laying of the foundation stone as follows. "Behind the sheer functional (...) there is the structurally interwoven – from the individual to the universal. (...) It is my duty with the Marl project to express structurally the extensive vocation of the school, as an image of full life."

The form of the plot enabled Scharoun to arrange the individual functional areas relatively free around a centre. This "room in the centre" takes up the large break hall and the assembly hall. At the same time it is the hinge between the administration area, the gymnasium and the classrooms for natural sciences on one side and the four class groups on the other side.

Like at Lünen each unit comprises four "school flats" (classroom, group room, lobby and external area). These are connected to a hall intended to serve for exhibitions and group activities. Circulating skylights light up the hexagonal classrooms. External areas with plants, linked by promenades, are assigned to the units of each age group. Thus varied outdoor rooms are created across the whole area.

1964–1971 ▸ German Embassy
Brasília, Brazil

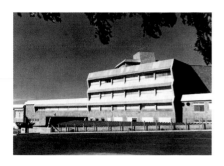

View of the office wing

The German Embassy in Brasília is the only project by Scharoun outside of Germany. On the one hand it may have something to do with his late international breakthrough. But it also corresponds to his inner attitude, which was more interested in form-making for a specific building project in a familiar situation than in universal or significant international architecture.

The building lies in the ambassadorial district of the new Brasilian capital city designed by Lucio Costa between the southern wing of the two-winged city floor plan (Plano Piloto) and the great artificial lake. Both parts, residence and chancellery, are put together in one block; a short distance away lie the dwellings for the staff. The curved floor plan of the main structure, an irregular U, is divided into both of its functional elements by a drive built over it. Following the drive one gets to the chancellery on the right hand and to the residence on the left.

The structure, with its recessed windows for climatic reasons, is characterised by a stepped graduation in height that imitates the topographical quality of the plot. The terracing enables an excellent view across the lake from each part of the building. In the garden as well, designed by well-known Brasilian landscape architect Roberto Burle Marx, the motif of terracing is continued.

The structural highlight of the complex is the reception rooms of the residence on the upper floor of the middle part. Here one finds a multi-layered interior roomscape with a series of ascending plateaus and fluid transitions, even to the garden of the embassy, typical of Scharoun. He intended, as he termed it, "to stage the course of festive events and personal meetings in innovative ways by abandoning traditional ideas of representation."

First floor plan
On the right is the office building; on the left is the residence

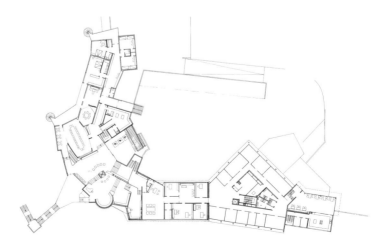

Left page:
The reception area of the residence shows a succession of rising plateaus.

1964–1978 ‣ National Library
Prussian Cultural Heritage Foundation
‣ Potsdamer Straße, Berlin

View from the National Gallery
The body of the structure is characterised by the massive storeroom, the "spine of a book". In front are the reading rooms and the lecture hall.

In 1964 Scharoun had won the library competition that was combined with a task of urban development, concerning the design of the space between National Library, the Philharmonic and the planned National Gallery by Ludwig Mies van der Rohe, opened in 1968. In later years this territory was known as the cultural forum.

The area between the three buildings was already predetermined by traffic planning. The much used Potsdamer Straße separates the Philharmonic and the National Gallery from the National Library. Scharoun attempts to visually moderate this break by a landscaped organisation of the masses of the building. A voluminous and stretched out part of the stockroom forms the backbone of the complex and has a protecting function eastward, where an urban autobahn was planned. Westward, oriented to the forum, the lower public sections of the library are loosely situated off the stockroom. The large reading room in the centre of these frontal parts of the building, with its two sides standing free, was shown in the competition design with a distinct formal reference as a kind of counterpart to the National Gallery. This reference was taken back in the built structure.

The public section extends over two levels: the generously-sized entrance zone with exhibition areas, as well as the long stretched band of three diversely subdivided reading rooms situated above. Two stairs positioned sideways serve the function of a link between both levels. At first they lead the visitors into the imposing east foyer that gives one an idea of the dimensions of the part of the stockroom that lies above. From this oversized mezzanine via three main stairs one gets to the reading rooms. The rectangular structures of the hall are twisted against each other in the familiar Scharounian manner and are defined as autonomous units. At the same time they are part of a fluid room, embracing the whole, which terraces down to the Kulturforum.

The National Library, Scharoun's Philharmonic and the New National Gallery by Mies van der Rohe were the main buildings of the cultural forum. Today the library is towered over by the neighbouring high-rise buildings on Potsdamer Platz. But Scharoun's largest building, approximately 230 metres long with its strikingly windowless stockroom, the "spine of a book", is still able to assert itself with superior ease in the changing surroundings. Planning took place in close collaboration with his colleague Edgar Wisniewski. The project had an unlucky history: there were considerable changes in the building programme. In 1969 the site supervision was taken away from Scharoun's office and limited to the artistic supervision. When in 1978, fourteen years after the competition and six years after Scharoun's death, the building could be opened, the substantial basic ideas nevertheless remained intact: "The idea carries," Scharoun had said in such cases.

Winding staircase in the general reading room

View into the general reading room

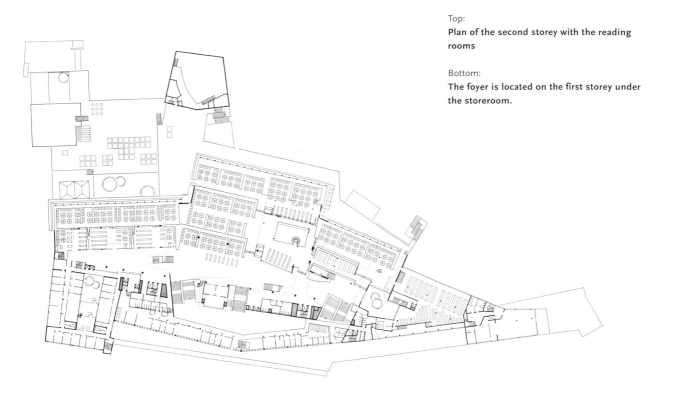

1965–1973 ▸ Municipal Theatre
Klieverhagen, Wolfsburg

Although Scharoun was engaged in studies and competitions with the building of theatres again and again during his long career, his Wolfsburg Municipal Theatre is the only one ever realised. It was inaugurated on October 5, 1973, almost a year after his death.

His concern with this subject can be traced back to the period of the "Gläserne Kette". There is a 1919 watercolour entitled "Reflections on new theatres", and in a 1921 lecture he was "concerned about modern stage design". From very early on he was concerned with the question of how the distance between the stage and the audience could be reduced and how to move the theatre, being a part of a more complex cultural building, "to the visible centre of the city." These were questions that even influenced the Wolfsburg design as well. After the Second World War Scharoun had intensely taken up the subject of theatre once more. In 1952 and 1953 he had considerably influenced the theatre debate of the post-war period by two often-discussed, inventive competition designs for the Kassel National Theatre and for the Mannheim National Theatre.

At the competition for the Wolfsburg theatre in 1965 Scharoun competed, among others, with Alvar Aalto and Jørn Utzon. The jury especially fell for his urban solution, because as in his designs for Kassel and Mannheim, he dealt here too with the special urban situation. The elongated structure, situated parallel to the slope of the Klieversberg mountain dominating the scenery, increases the topographical quality somewhat, quite in accordance with the expressionist idea of a "Stadtkrone". Meanwhile the originally existing visual link to the city centre with the City Hall and the cultural centre by Alvar Aalto has been blocked by new buildings.

Right:
Theatre hall

Left page:
The distribution of the visitors is put in the limelight with excitement in the front room of the theatre hall.

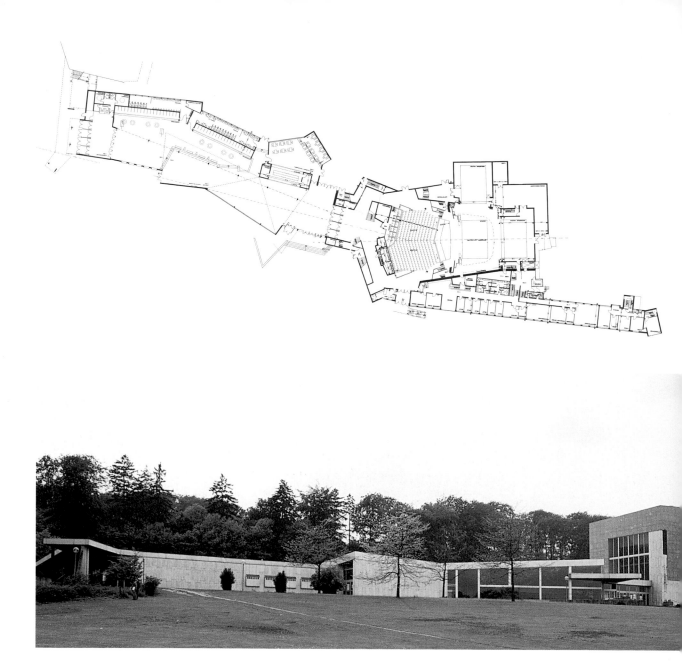

The total view from the east
The lengthy body stands impressively in front of the wooded top of the mountain.

The structure is composed of three elements: the irregular polygon of the building with the hall and stage towering above everything as well as two flat wings. In the west wing there is the administration area, and in the east wing there is an unusually long foyer zone with vast panoramic windows, looking to the city centre. The foyer serves the function of an exhibition room and is used for festive receptions.

The path of the visitor leads through the entire length of this foyer zone, about 80 metres. One enters a narrow gate and then the lobby, a room that is unusually high and surprises the visitor with its natural lighting. Through a large window above the gate, daylight comes into the lobby, which is part of the auditorium, as it is shown by the

Left page:
Ground floor plan
On the left is the foyer zone; in the middle are the hall and the stage building; on the right is the administrative section.

Right, top:
Entrance area
In the background are the hall and the stage building.

Right, bottom:
Entrance area with garage access

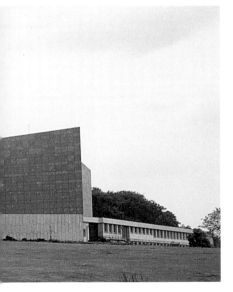

continuous transition of the ceiling and the central view. Here Scharoun suspensefully stages the distribution of visitors. The lobby becomes the threshold between the imaginary site of the stage and the outside world. Scharoun even accepted acoustic disadvantages for the sake of this room impression.

1969–1975 ▸ German Maritime Museum

Hans-Scharoun-Platz, Bremerhaven

Main entrance

Stairway to the "Cog House"

Initially, a private initiative sponsored the conception for a German Maritime Museum in Bremerhaven, in which, among other things, the Cog of the Hanseatic league, excavated in 1962 in Bremen, was to be exhibited. In 1969 the plan got a decisive turn after Hans Scharoun could be secured as architect.

The proposition was fortunate for two reasons. On the one hand hardly any other architect of modernism had sought so many formal and constructive-functional loans during ship-building. One the other hand, Scharoun had grown up in Bremerhaven, very close to the location of the museum at the old harbour. In his old age, the task led him back to "the place of origin ... of that creative motivation which has sustained me throughout my life," as he termed it in his explanation.

The building follows two given lines, the Weser dyke and the old harbour that serves as a harbour for the museum. Whereas the administration wing runs parallel to the dike, the "Cog House" and the adjoining exhibitions spaces are oriented to the harbour basin. The halls for special exhibitions and the lecture hall mediate between both directions. The exhibition area is characterised by fluid transitions between the individual sections. The visitor is discretely guided on a tour through the building, yet is free to choose his own route instead. Inner points of reference are the focused stairwell flooded with light and a high exhibition hall, where the centre part of a river paddle steamer is set up. Skilfully placed windows always serve as a visual relation to the maritime surroundings.

A pilot-bridge-like superstructure, into which, as a matter of fact, an original pilot-bridge is incorporated, leads to a ship association with this building as with some other buildings by Scharoun. Scharoun's original intention, to lead a public passage through the museum, starting at the dike over a bridge to the hall and on to the harbour of the museum, could not be done for organisational reasons.

Left page:
The museum is bordered by the Weser dike and the museum harbour.

Topping out ceremony for the National Gallery by Mies van der Rohe
In the foreground, starting at the right: Scharoun, Mies van der Rohe, Scharoun's second wife Margit, in the back Wassili Luckhardt.

1943–1945 ▶ Activities for the building control department Steglitz in the removal of bomb damages

1945–1946 ▶ After the war Scharoun is offered by the Allies the posts of City councillor as well as head of the building and housing department of the city authorities of Berlin. He presented his urban concept for the post-war Berlin in the exhibition "Berlin plant".

1946–1958 ▶ Professor at the faculty of architecture of the Berlin Technical University, chair and head of Institute for Urban Development

1947–1950 ▶ Head of the "Institute for Building Industry" at the German Academy of Sciences in Berlin

1949 ▶ Competion for the Liederhalle in Stuttgart (1st prize)

1951 ▶ Draft of a basic primary and secondary school for the "Darmstadt Talks"

1952–1954 ▶ Competition for National Theatre design in Kassel (1st prize)

1954–1959 ▶ Complex of residential high-rises "Romeo and Juliet", Stuttgart-Zuffenhausen

1954–1961 ▶ Housing estate Charlottenburg-Nord in Berlin

1955 ▶ Urban competition Bürgerweide in Bremen (1st prize)

1955–1962 ▶ Geschwister-Scholl school in Lünen

1955–1968 ▶ President of the Academy of the Arts, Berlin

1956–1963 ▶ Philharmonic in Berlin

1959–1963 ▶ Residential high-rise "Salute" in Stuttgart-Fasanenhof

1960 ▶ Marriage with Margit von Plato

1960–1971 ▶ School building in Marl

1962–1970 ▶ Institutes of the Faculty of Architecture, Berlin Technical University

1963–1966 ▶ Housing estate "Rauher Kapf" in Böblingen

1964–1971 ▶ Embassy building of the Federal Republic of Germany in Brasília, Brazil

1964–1978 ▶ National Library of the Prussian Cultural Heritage Foundation in Berlin

1965 ▶ Auguste-Perret prize of the Union Internationale des Architectes, Paris

1965–1973 ▶ Municipal Theatre, Wolfsburg

1966 ▶ Johannes chapel of the Christian Community in Bochum

1968 ▶ Honorary president of the Academy of the Arts, Berlin

1969–1975 ▶ German Maritime Museum in Bremerhaven

1971 ▶ Residential high-rise "Orplid" in Böblingen

1972 ▶ Hans Scharoun dies November 25 at the age of 79 in Berlin.

Germany

Bibliography

Credits

▶ Arndt, Adolf: Demokratie als Bauherr, in: Ingeborg Flagge, Wolfgang Jean Stock (ed.): Bauen und Demokratie. Ostfildern-Ruit, 1992

▶ Bartning, Otto (ed.): Mensch und Raum Darmstadt, 1952. New edition: Mensch und Raum. Das Darmstädter Gespräch 1951. Brunswick, 1991

▶ Behne, Adolf: Der moderne Zweckbau. New edition, Frankfurt/M., 1964

▶ Blundell Jones, Peter: Hans Scharoun. London, 1995

▶ Bürkle, J. Christoph: Hans Scharoun. Zurich, 1993

▶ Geist, Johann Friedrich and Klaus Kürvers: Das Berliner Mietshaus 1945 – 1989. Munich, 1989

▶ Geist, Johann Friedrich, Klaus Kürvers, Dieter Rausch: Hans Scharoun. Chronik zu Leben und Werk, Berlin 1993

▶ Hoh-Slodczyk, Christine et. al.: Hans Scharoun. Architekt in Deutschland 1893 – 1972, Munich, 1992

▶ Janofske, Eckehard: Architektur-Räume. Idee und Gestalt bei Hans Scharoun, Braunschweig 1984

▶ Joedicke, Jürgen: Architekturgeschichte des 20. Jahrhunderts. Von 1950 bis zur Gegenwart. Stuttgart, 1990

▶ Kirschenmann, Jörg C. and Eberhard Syring: Hans Scharoun. Die Forderung des Unvollendeten. Stuttgart, 1993

▶ Lepik, Andres und Anne Schmedding: Architektur in Berlin. Das XX. Jahrhundert – ein Jahrhundert Kunst in Deutschland. Cologne, 1999

▶ Pehnt, Wolfgang: Die Architektur des Expressionismus. Stuttgart ,1973

▶ Pfankuch, Peter (ed.): Hans Scharoun. Bauten, Entwürfe, Texte. New edition, Berlin, 1993

▶ Posener, Julius: Vorlesungen zur Geschichte der neuen Architektur (1), Arch+. Aachen, 1983

▶ Risselada. Max (ed.): Funktionalismus 1927 – 1961. Hans Scharoun versus die Opbouw. Sulgen, 1999

▶ Wendschuh, Achim (ed.): Hans Scharoun. Zeichnungen, Aquarelle, Texte. Berlin, 1993

▶ Wisniewski, Edgar: Die Berliner Philharmonie und ihr Kammermusiksaal. Der Konzertsaal als Zentralraum. Berlin, 1993